Symbols of America

Written by Susan A. DeStefano

Table of Contents

We live in a free and beautiful country.

The story of how America became a free country makes us feel proud. **Symbols** like the flag and the eagle remind us how important our freedom is. They also make us think about what it means to be Americans.

U.S. Constitution

Rocky Mountains

Symbols can send
a message without
using words. Let's
find out more about
our flag and other
American symbols.

The Liberty Bell

The Liberty Bell is a symbol of **freedom**. Hundreds of years ago, it rang out to call people to come and hear the first reading of the Declaration of Independence.

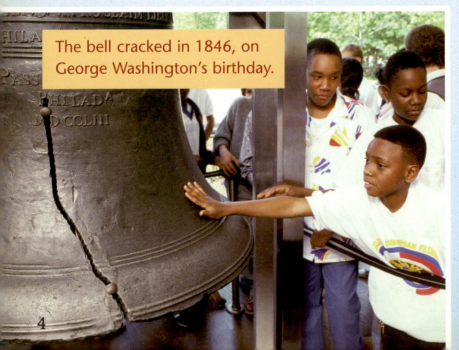

The bell cracked in 1846, on George Washington's birthday.

At last, the king of England could no longer tell us what to do. Today we still celebrate the same message the bell rang out in 1776—America is a free country.

Fourth of July fireworks

The American Flag

After America became a free country, we needed a new flag. The first flag had 13 stars—one for each of the first 13 states. Today there are 50 states, so there are 50 stars on the flag.

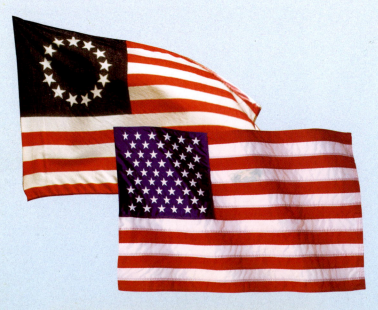

Today's flag still has one stripe for each of the thirteen original states.

Fourth of July parade

American astronaut on the moon

The flag reminds us that we are all Americans **united** together as one people.

The Bald Eagle

The bald eagle became our national bird while we were still fighting for our freedom. Our leaders wanted a symbol that said Americans were strong and brave. Can you see why they chose the bald eagle?

bald eagle

Ben Franklin thought the bald eagle was a mean bird and a terrible choice for our national symbol. His choice was a proud and majestic bird—the wild turkey.

The
Statue of Liberty

The Statue of Liberty is an amazing sight. As one of the tallest statues in the world, she has welcomed millions of **immigrants** to America.

Immigrants entering America wait in line at Ellis Island for a ferry that will take them to New York City.

She is a symbol of hope and freedom. Her message is: Here you will be free and have a chance for a better life.

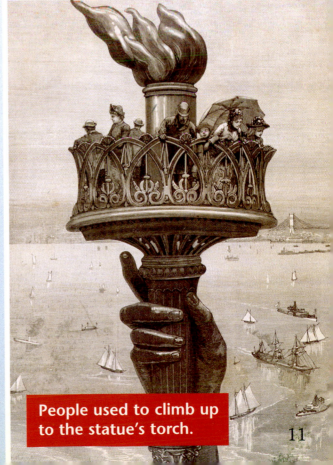

People used to climb up to the statue's torch.

11

Washington, D.C.

Washington, D.C., is the **capital** of the United States. It is where the president lives and where our nation's laws are made.

More than any other American city, it symbolizes our country, our history, and our government.

The president and his staff work in the White House.

Congress makes our laws inside the Capitol Building.

Washington is a beautiful city that all Americans can be proud of. It has many monuments and museums to remind us of our country's past. If you visit Washington, D.C., here are just a few of the things you can see.

Washington Monument

Every spring, Washington, D.C., welcomes the beauty of its cherry trees at the National Cherry Blossom Festival. Many of these trees were a gift from Japan.

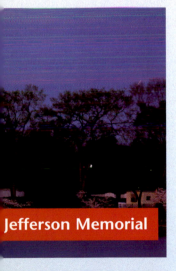

Jefferson Memorial

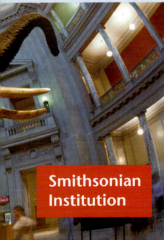

Smithsonian Institution

Lincoln Memorial

If you could choose a new symbol of America, what would it be? What message would you want it to send?